Old Fochabers
with Lhanbryde, Urquhart, Garmouth, Kingston a
Douglas G. Lockhart

Each summer the Territorial battalions in the north of Scotland spent a fortnight at a training camp. In this photograph taken on 12 June 1909, E Company of the 6th Seaforth Highlanders can be seen marching to Fochabers Town Station where they made the short journey, changing at Alves Junction, to reach Burghead (see *Old Burghead, Cummingston and Hopeman*, Stenlake Publishing). There they joined their battalion and, along with three more battalions, numbered 1,500 men. They spent the next two weeks drilling, on live firing practice, skirmishing and engaging in a mock battle that involved regular troops of the 2nd Seaforths who were assigned to both sides and provided training.

1

The formation of a golf course at Spey Bay in the early 1900s involved support from many communities in the local area. On 11 October 1906 the *Banffshire Advertiser* described how Ben Sayers of North Berwick had '… marked off what he assured the directors would be a first class professional course when made'. The official opening took place on 10 September 1907 when the Duke of Richmond and Gordon's son, Lord Walter Gordon Lennox, played the opening tee shot while watched by 3,000 spectators. Spey Bay quickly established itself as a golfing centre and its tournament weeks were very popular. The links character of the course can be seen in this photograph of an unknown lady golfer preparing to drive at the third hole in 1928. The course became well known during the inter-war period thanks to the support of Ramsay MacDonald, Britain's first Labour prime minister, when he was holidaying at Lossiemouth.

© Douglas G. Lockart, 2017
First published in the United Kingdom, 2017,
by Stenlake Publishing Ltd.
www.stenlake.co.uk
ISBN 978-1-84033-791-4

The publishers regret that they cannot supply
copies of any pictures featured in this book.

Printed by
Blissetts, Roslin Road, Acton, W3 8DH

Acknowledgements

I would like to thank the staffs of Aberdeen City and Aberdeenshire Archives; Special Collections Centre, University of Aberdeen; Elgin Library; National Library of Scotland, Edinburgh; National Records of Scotland, Edinburgh; and Carnegie Library, Ayr for their help with my enquiries.

Further Reading

The websites and books listed below were used by the author during his research. None of them are available from Stenlake Publishing. Those interested in discovering more are advised to visit Elgin Library or the National Library of Scotland which have comprehensive collections of local history books, maps and newspapers.

Anderson, G., *Kingston-on-Spey*, Oliver and Boyd, Edinburgh, 1957.
Bulloch, J.M. (ed.), *The Gordon Book*, Rosemount Press, Aberdeen, 1902.
Hamilton, H. (ed.), The Counties of Moray and Nairn, *The Third Statistical Account*, Vol. 17, Collins, Glasgow, 1965.
Lockhart, D.G., *Scottish Planned Villages*, Scottish History Society, Edinburgh, 2012.
Lockhart, D.G., 'Gordon Castle Fête, 6 September 1916', *Scottish Local History*, 96, 2017, pp.23-5.
McKean, C., *The District of Moray: An Illustrated Architectural Guide*, RIAS, Edinburgh, 1987.
Northern Scot Christmas Number 1921 p.18 [photographs of the Lhanbryde and Garmouth War Memorials].
Skelton, J., *Speybuilt: The story of a forgotten industry*, W. Skelton, Garmouth, 2nd ed., 1995.
Walker, D.W. and Woodworth, M., *The Buildings of Scotland, Aberdeenshire: North and Moray*, Yale University Press, New Haven and London, 2015.
Watson, J. & W., *Morayshire Described*, Russell and Watson, Elgin, 1868.
Withrington, D. J. and Grant I.R. (eds.), *The Statistical Account of Scotland 1791–1799 edited by Sir John Sinclair*, Vol. 16: Banffshire, Moray and Nairnshire, EP Publishing, Wakefield, 1982.
The New Statistical Account of Scotland, Vol. 13; Banff, Elgin and Nairn (1845): www.electricscotland.com/history/statistical/volume13.html
Ordnance Survey maps provided by the National Library of Scotland: www.maps.nls.uk/os/index.html

Introduction

This book is in two sections. The first part is a photographic guide to Fochabers and nearby Gordon Castle which was the Scottish seat of the Dukes of Richmond and Gordon. In the second part the photographs of the smaller communities to the north and west have been arranged as a journey beginning in Lhanbryde and then Urquhart before heading for the coast near the mouth of the River Spey, the location of the former maritime communities of Garmouth and Kingston. Finally, we cross to the opposite bank of the river and explore the hamlet of Spey Bay.

Although located within a short distance of each other, the places in this book all have quite different characteristics. Fochabers is a fine example of a new town designed by the architect John Baxter of Edinburgh in the 1770s in the manner of Inveraray, Argyllshire, and Cullen, Banffshire, to replace an older settlement that was in decay and too close to the laird's castle. Around the same time, Gordon Castle was rebuilt to become one of the greatest country houses in northern Scotland while its policies boasted a landscaped park, a lake and a walled garden. The impressive main entrance was at the West Lodge between the new town and the River Spey. Fochabers acquired all the features that were typical of the more successful planned villages of the period: a main street intersected by lesser streets at right angles thus forming a grid pattern; a large square with two-storey housing, an inn and an imposing church – Bellie Parish Church was relocated to the new town – so that by the 1841 Census the population totalled 1,135. The town benefited from the patronage of the Dukes of Gordon (later Richmond and Gordon) who were responsible for improving the water supply and introducing electricity, events that were commemorated by a fountain and a decorative lamp in the Square. New public buildings appeared in Victorian and Edwardian times, funded by private benefactors and local fund raising, such as Milne's School, the Pringle Memorial Church and the Public Institute. However, during the inter-war period the deaths in quick succession of the 7th and 8th Dukes led to the sale in 1937 of the Gordon Castle estates to the Crown. The family moved out of the castle the following year and the furniture and fittings were auctioned. The castle and policies were bought by one of the grandsons of the 7th Duke in 1953, however much demolition took place and only the central tower, the east wing and part of the west wing survived.

The Earls of Fife owned estates west of Fochabers and two planned villages with quite different origins were established on these lands. Urquhart dates from 1783–84 and originally consisted of a single street of cottages flanked by lots of land attached to each cottage, providing opportunities for subsistence farming. The people became very dependent on their lots and ten years later they petitioned the laird for more land. The village was characterised by single-storey cottages and the population had only grown to 185 by the 1841 Census. In contrast Lhanbryde was remodelled in the early 1850s with architect-designed cottages arranged in terraces on either side of the main Elgin–Fochabers road; it became a desirable place to live and in the early twentieth century attracted retired people.

Garmouth is located on higher ground overlooking the River Spey, with the village spilling down towards the river. It was a trading port in the medieval period, raised in status to a burgh of barony in 1587, and had a harbour, market cross and rights to hold two annual fairs. The wood trade at the harbour was described in 1798 'as the most considerable, it is supposed, for home timber in Scotland' and was mainly responsible for the town's wealth, evidence of which can be seen in its fine eighteenth and early nineteenth century houses. About a mile north is Kingston, another former port and centre of the timber trade. In 1784 two timber merchants from Hull purchased the Glenmore Forest and began floating timber down the Spey. Merchants and shipbuilders took advantage of supplies of fir trees to set up saw mills and shipyards. The impact of these activities can be seen in the numbers involved in shipbuilding, ship owning and men who went to sea. Despite massive damage along the Spey in the Great Flood of 1829, the industry continued to grow until the late 1860s after which competition from iron-hulled ships led to a steady decline in the fortunes of Garmouth and Kingston. By the time the photographs in this book were taken in the early twentieth century shipbuilding had ceased and the population of both places had shrunk from their peak in 1861. In contrast Spey Bay on the east bank of the river only began to develop after the opening of the Richmond Hotel and a golf course in 1907. Although it was in an out of the way location Spey Bay nevertheless became a fashionable place to relax and play golf during the summer months.

The Fochabers Town branch left the main line between Keith and Elgin at Orbliston Junction, seen here in 1930. The branch, which opened in 1893 with a service of six trains in each direction, was built by the Highland Railway as a response to the opening in 1886 of the Banffshire Coast Railway by the Great North of Scotland Railway, which served Fochabers Station (later called Spey Bay), four miles north of the village itself. However, Fochabers Town station was handicapped by its location in Mosstodloch on the west bank of the River Spey about a mile from the village because bridging the river to bring the terminus closer to town would have been very expensive.

FOCHABERS

Passenger services to Fochabers Town began on 23 October 1893. The opening was celebrated in style with a procession along the High Street and through the Gordon Castle grounds to the station which lay on the west bank of the Spey. The first train to Obliston Junction consisted of two locomotives and eighteen carriages and carried 1,300 people. Fireworks in the square in the evening and a ball at the Temperance Hall completed the programme of events. Passenger services to Fochabers Town ceased on 14 September 1931 along with those on the branch between Alves Junction, Burghead and Hopeman (see *Old Burghead, Cummingston and Hopeman*, Stenlake Publishing). The *Elgin Courant and Courier* of 28 August explained that this was due to 'the stiff bus competition of recent years'. Freight traffic continued to Fochabers until March 1966. The once attractive station building, which incorporated the Duke's waiting room, looks neglected in this photograph taken in June 1960, remarkably however it was restored as semi-detached houses and can be found in Inchberry Place, surrounded by modern housing.

Crofts of Dipple, Fochabers

The Crofts of Dipple are a long line of mainly single-storey cottages on the west side of the B9105 south of Mosstodloch, an area where crofts were the typical landholding. The inhabitants were farm servants, labourers and, as might be expected with the River Spey not far away, salmon fishers. A blacksmith was recorded in every census between 1841 and 1901 and the smithy, which dates from the mid-nineteenth century, is a listed building. The cottages can still be seen today, albeit much modernised.

The foundation stone of the Boat-of-Bog bridge over the River Spey at Fochabers was laid by the Marquis of Huntly in June 1801 and was completed a little over three years later. Unfortunately, the western pier and the two arches that it supported were destroyed in the Moray floods of 1829. The bridge re-opened in 1832 after the foundations of the central pier were strengthened and a timber arch installed in the gap. This proved to be a short-term solution as dry rot was discovered in the timber in 1853 and it was replaced by the cast-iron version which can be seen in the photograph. The *Third Statistical Account* in 1954 noted increasing road traffic but it was not until July 1972 that a new bridge over the River Spey, parallel to the first, was opened, intended as the first stage of a bypass of Fochabers. Another forty years would elapse until the much debated bypass would be completed.

Burnbank is situated on the northern edge of Fochabers, close to where the Fochabers Burn flows into the River Spey. The Gas Works, which was built in 1841 at the height of the 'gas mania' in the North East, was located here though this closed after the introduction of electricity in 1905 from a small hydro scheme that used the swift flowing waters of the Spey. The housing scheme was built in 1948 and 1949 and by the latter year 28 typically three-bedroom houses were occupied. A further four houses were added in 1953. Although council housing provided a standard of accommodation which many older properties lacked, commentators at the time felt that future generations might be less happy about their appearance. Although Burnbank may not possess the charm of the streets in the planned village, criticism of social housing in Moray has mainly been directed towards the larger more recent developments such as those near Lhanbryde.

FOCHABERS

A site for an inn was a priority in planning the new town. However, the earliest advertisement for the Gordon Arms Hotel is in the *Aberdeen Journal* of 6 July 1803 although the building itself dates from the late 1770s. The advertisement advised readers that, 'The House, Stables, &c. have undergone a thorough repair; the cellars are properly supplied; the lodgings are newly refitted; and no expence [sic] has been spared in order to make everything comfortable to the traveller'. The house opposite is another late eighteenth century property which has had shop windows added. It was occupied by the firm of R. and J. Innes, tailors, who had the patronage of Gordon Castle. After the death of Robert Innes in 1909, ownership of the house passed to his daughter Amy and the business was run by Mitchell Suttie of Coatbridge. The shop is a hairdresser's today.

A.2571. SQUARE AND HIGH STREET, FOCHABERS.

Not only an attractively planned town, Fochabers also became a significant commercial centre. It had several bakeries, many small firms in the building trades, a blacksmith's, a large garage, a range of shops, two banks and two hotels. Many of these businesses were located in the Square and along the main street. In addition, Baxter's foods – located less than a mile away on the opposite side of the River Spey – had grown from its roots as a small shop to a major industry that employed around 150 people in 1950.

FOCHABERS

Winters in Victorian times were colder than today as the ice-clad fountain and the popularity of curling as a winter pastime confirm. The fountain in the Square was built by the people of Fochabers in 1878 to commemorate the introduction of piped water which was supplied to standpipes. The attached plaque acknowledges '... the liberality of the Sixth Duke of Richmond and Gordon K.G. in supplying water to the town'. In the background are some of the fine two-storey houses that are a feature of the Square. The grocer's shop visible to the left of the fountain was run by Margaret Grant (1852–1934), the sign 'Refreshments' suggesting that there was demand from passing trade on the main thoroughfare through the town.

The Lamp in the Square was erected in 1906 to commemorate the introduction of electricity generated by a hydro-electric scheme pioneered by the Duke of Richmond and Gordon. A canal was dug that tapped water from the River Spey, which was then led to two turbines at the mouth of the Fochabers Burn. The switching-on ceremony took place in November 1905. Also in the photograph, at the top of Duke Street is Gordon Chapel (Scottish Episcopal Church) which was originally a private chapel for the castle. It is an example of Gothic revival architecture, designed by Archibald Simpson (1790–1847) of Aberdeen in 1832 and opened two years later. The Rectory, once an Episcopalian school, is on the lower floor while the church is upstairs.

The Lamp, Fochabers

FOCHABERS

The Square was the centrepiece of John Baxter's plan for the new town and it was only to be expected that the Duke of Gordon should commission him to design the elegant Bellie Church to replace the dilapidated old kirk near the graveyard to the north of the Gordon Castle policies. An advertisement for tradesmen to tender for the building work was placed in the *Aberdeen Journal* on 27 November 1786. The resulting church has been described as 'impressive', the 'crown jewel' and 'a building that would be ornamental to any city in Europe'. This vista can still be enjoyed today though for over forty years it was spoiled by a bus shelter and public toilets which were only demolished after a referendum was held in 1995.

FOCHABERS

Huntly Street, Fochabers.

This section of the main street is typical of the range of small businesses that could be found in Fochabers in the early 1930s. On the right are Isabella and Jane Mitchell, drapers, James Bonnyman, shoemaker, and E.M. Thom, grocer but also advertising hairdressing, teas and ice-creams! On the left, on the margin of the photograph, is the shop of William Murray & Sons, bakers. The Grant Arms Hotel at the junction with Westmoreland Street was described by the *Northern Scot* at the time of the death of its owner (John Grant, 1823–82) as a 'fine new hotel'. Opposite the car in the middle distance is the garage premises owned by John Slorach (1872–1942), engineer, that was housed in a corrugated iron shed. In the early 1930s it was rented by different motor engineers and by the end of the decade it had become Hampton's Garage, adorned by signs advertising tyres and oil and able to offer a choice of fuel from Shell and Esso. Beyond is the Pringle Memorial Church, built from the legacy of Alexander Pringle (1816–96), a native of Fochabers. The memorial stone was laid in July 1899 and the church was opened on 21 December 1900.

HIGH STREET, FOCHABERS   D 4331

This postcard covers much the same ground as the previous one but was taken twenty years later. The grocer's shop in the view had belonged to Lipp & Son, which on the retirement of John Lipp (1852–1939) had been purchased by James Thomson (1890–1948), who had served an apprenticeship with the firm and whose trustees were owners in the 1950s. Another difference is the growth of motor traffic which would continue to increase during the next sixty years before the opening of a bypass offered some relief. A less visible change occurred when the congregations of the Pringle Memorial Church and Bellie Parish Church were united in 1947. After protracted negotiations it was agreed that the Pringle Church would become the church hall and services would continue in the Parish Church. In the early 1980s the Pringle Hall became surplus to requirements and was converted into Fochabers Heritage Centre. It was officially opened by the Lord Lieutenant of Morayshire, Captain Iain Tennant, on 24 June 1984.

A public institute that would be a memorial to the Duchess of Richmond was proposed in 1887, however a memorial cairn was built on the summit of Whiteash Hill south-east of the town instead. The original project was revived as a reading room in 1900 and fund raising began. A bazaar was held in the gardens of Gordon Castle in September 1902 and shortly after the Duke donated a site on the High Street near Milne's High School. There was a further financial windfall when Andrew Carnegie offered a donation of £1,000 for a free library. The public hall and institute opened on 27 October 1905 and to celebrate the occasion the band of the Black Watch played during an evening of entertainment that included songs and amateur dramatics. The Institute has been a much treasured asset; its jubilee in 1955 was marked by six days of celebration and fund-raising initiatives to maintain and modernise the building continue to this day.

FOCHABERS

Alexander Milne was a servant at Gordon Castle, who having refused to cut and powder his hair and thus incurring the wrath of his employer, emigrated to America, and became a wealthy merchant, slave owner and manufacturer in New Orleans. He bequeathed $100,000 on his death in 1838 to endow a school to provide free education for children in his home town and parish. However, Milne's will was contested in America and several years elapsed before funds were released. Built in a Tudor-Gothic style to a design by Elgin architect Thomas Mackenzie, the school was officially opened on 16 November 1846. More recently, the school witnessed another long running dispute when the community opposed Moray Council's plans for a new primary school on a green-field site. However, on 21 May 1993, the *Northern Scot* announced a 'Village victory in new-school battle' which was followed by conversion work so that Fochabers Primary School could occupy this historic building.

FOCHABERS

SOUTH STREET, FOCHABERS   D 7105

Photographs of the main streets and squares of the planned villages of the North East are very common, back streets and lanes much less so. The plan of Fochabers contains two streets, one on each side of the Main Street. In South Street (previously South Row) there are a number of attractive houses and it has been the location of two churches, St Mary's Roman Catholic Church set back from the trees on the right (page 18) and the Free Church was about half way along the street until it was replaced by the Pringle Memorial Church in the High Street in December 1900 (pages 13 and 14). The gardens of the houses are across the street and have an uninterrupted southerly aspect.

The attractive St Mary Catholic Church with its prominent finials and three Gothic windows is situated in South Street. Construction began in 1826 and it can accommodate around 400 worshippers. Before it was built the congregation worshipped in a house in the village. The interior impressed a reporter of the *Northern Scot* during his survey of the rural kirks of Moray in 1924. He spoke of 'Wonderfully decorated walls, beautiful paintings, magnificent architecture, an artistic censer, and pleasing sculpture work meet the eye'. Just over twenty years ago there was a major fund-raising appeal for the chapel's restoration fund. A sale held on 30 November 1994 at the Public Institute echoed back to the age of the bazaar with prominent church-goers contributing gifts to be auctioned and entertainment and dancing in the evening.

A 2565

Fochabers from the South East.

The spires of the Parish Church (left) and Pringle Memorial Church (right) are prominent landmarks in this photograph. In the foreground gardeners at Christie's nursery can be seen at work. Thomas Christie (*c.* 1795–1868) acquired the site near the junction of the Keith and Cullen roads in 1820 from the last Duke of Gordon and set about reclaiming the boggy moorland. The nursery was enlarged by his son, William (1851–1921), who extended the business throughout the North East and to customers as far afield as Stranraer, Kilmarnock and Coldstream. During the chairmanship of George William Christie (1926–2007) the nursery became the largest supplier of forest tree seedlings to private woodland owners. The business also diversified its interests with shops in Elgin, Buckie, Keith and Fochabers and also three hotels. The garden centre has now become a significant tourist destination.

FOCHABERS

Old Gordon Castle featured several towers. An engraving of the castle by John Slezer from around 1672 can be seen in many architectural guide books. In 1769 Alexander, 4th Duke of Gordon, commissioned John Baxter of Edinburgh to redevelop the site on a massive scale. Only the south-east tower of the old castle was retained and this was incorporated into a four-storey central block flanked by two-storey links to two-storey pavilions and courtyards. The resulting façade was 538 feet long. In this photograph, taken of the north side of the castle, the scale of the central block is evident, dwarfing the adjacent east pavilion and its service wing and court. Partly hidden by the tree is the west wing which was designed by Baxter as a coach house and stables.

Major Allan Wilson, a native of Fochabers who was educated at Milne's Institution and for a time was a clerk in the Town and Country Bank branch, lost his life along with other members of his patrol on the banks of the Shangani River in Matabeleland in Zimbabwe (formerly Southern Rhodesia) in December 1893. Steps were taken as early as February 1894 to raise funds for a memorial and an early suggestion was a memorial hall, reading room and library, while another was the erection of an obelisk. However, by September opinion had shifted in favour of a water fountain. The successful design, chosen by the Duke of Richmond and Gordon, was by William Kirkland Cutlar (1864–1942), an architect of Forres. The fountain was built opposite the West Lodge, the main entrance to Gordon Castle, and was unveiled on 18 October 1895.

GORDON CASTLE, FOCHABERS

This view of the south facing façade was taken from the south-east corner of the formal garden and shows one of the two large fountains from which paths radiated. Behind the fountain is the orangery with its large full-height windows, dating from *c.* 1830, and beyond it are the east pavilion and its service wing, both of which survived the partial demolition of the castle in 1953.

Gordon Castle

This photograph which looks north along the Broad Walk, was taken from the Broad Steps which was part of the walking route for the family from the castle to the Episcopal Chapel in the village. The castle was a Voluntary Aid Hospital for convalescing soldiers during the First World War and in the next conflict it housed soldiers. The Crown Estates Commissioners, which had bought the estate in 1937, sold the site of the castle and part of the policies and gardens to Colonel George Gordon Lennox, grandson of the 7th Duke, who demolished parts of the castle in 1953. The east wing is now a hotel owned by the Gordon Lennox family and the residual buildings in the west wing are used for farming.

GORDON CASTLE

The Duchess Tree, Gordon Castle

Many of the reports of the fête in the newspapers in September 1916 comment on the attractiveness of the castle policies. The *Nairnshire Telegraph* noted that the '… magnificent trees in varied foliage … were for many the chief attraction. The famous Duchess's Tree, which is some hundreds of years old and has rooted its branches all round, was the object of a special visit'. When this photograph was taken about 1905 the lime tree which was located a short distance south-west of the castle gardens had a girth of around seventeen feet when measured five feet from ground level. It was a casualty of the severe storm which swept southwards over the North Sea on 31 January 1953.

The Quarry Garden can be found in the northern part of the policies, off the track that leads to Quarry Garden Lodge and then Bellie Lodge on the Spey Bay road (B9104). The entrance is beneath a bridge and just beyond it are hidden gardens that were developed in an old red sandstone quarry by Elizabeth, the 5th and last Duchess of Gordon. These feature terraced slopes planted with evergreen shrubs, a Grecian Temple folly and a fountain which was added in 1902. The visitor's guide *Morayshire Described*, published in 1868, suggested that this was 'one of the most delightful spots … and no visitors to Gordon Castle should finish their tour of inspection without having seen it'. Today, the gardens are overgrown and the circular base of a fountain is the only structure still visible.

GORDON CASTLE

The Fochabers Curling Club was founded in 1870 and enjoyed the patronage of successive Dukes of Richmond and Gordon. The lake in the castle grounds was a popular venue for curling and also attracted skaters from Fochabers. Describing conditions during the previous winter, the *Banffshire Advertiser* of 8 December 1881 stated that '… the crowds of skaters had occasionally to cut so close upon the curlers as to render it somewhat uncomfortable for both'. To remedy this a new curling pond, seen here, was built on flat land below the lake. The club was active until the outbreak of the Second World War, after which the pond fell into disuse. Today it is dry, the curlers' hut has gone and the only clues in the landscape are low embankments, a sluice gate and an overflow channel.

GORDON CASTLE

The St Andrews Lhanbryde Public School, Parish Church and Manse were situated at Sheriffston close to the B9103 road, about one mile west of Lhanbryde village. Following the 1872 Education (Scotland) Act one of the earliest decisions of the new school board was to engage Elgin-born architect Alexander Marshall Mackenzie (1848–1933) to make plans for an addition to the school buildings, costing about £600 and accommodating 70 children. The schoolmaster (pictured) was Robert Stephen (1843–1910) who took up the post in 1871, having previously been at Auchindoir, Aberdeenshire. He was regarded by his peers as the 'father' of his profession in Morayshire. Further improvements to the school buildings were made in 1907: an additional school room and a porch were added and by this time the school roll had almost doubled to around 135 pupils. The school continued to serve the village until the mid-1960s when a new school on the Garmouth road in Lhanbryde was opened. St Andrews School became a special school and the buildings were last used in 2002. When visited by this author in September 2016 the school was in a derelict condition.

LHANBRYDE

Lhanbryde was re-modelled from an earlier village in the early 1850s. It differs from most planned villages in the North East because the houses were designed by professional architects – Thomas Mackenzie (1814–54) and James Matthews (1819–98) – and the properties had front gardens, creating a pleasant suburban environment. On 28 March 1851 an advertisement in the *Elgin Courant* invited estimates 'FOR the MASON, CARPENTER, SLATER, PLUMBER, and MASON WORKS of a number of NEW COTTAGES, to be built for the VILLAGE of LHANBRYDE'. In November a similar notice for a new inn was published and the foundation stone was laid on 24 March 1852. It became the Fife Arms Hotel, a coaching inn which can be seen in the middle distance and on the next page. However, after the business was acquired by James George in 1927 it was renamed the Tennant Arms Hotel to reflect changing local landownership following the break-up of the Fife Estates.

LHANBRYDE

West-End, Lhanbryde.

This photograph shows the opposite direction to the view on the previous page. Two small shops can be seen on the left, the closer one being the butcher's shop occupied since 1973 by Robert George although it dates back to the 1920s. It replaced an earlier one at the rear of the feu and bridges the gap between adjacent cottages. Next door is the post office. On the opposite side of the road is the grocery shop of James Scott (1880–1958), a shepherd's son who was born in Enzie, Banffshire. Scott began his business in 1908 and was the first to offer a motor van service in 1915. He retired in 1945 and the business was sold to the Scottish Co-operative Wholesale Society. The Co-op closed in 1970 and was acquired by the adjacent Tennant Arms Hotel, which built a rectangular flat roofed extension to accommodate a new bar area. The hotel closed down about 10 years ago.

Again looking west from slightly further along St Andrew's Road, the main interest is the entrance to Lhanbryde Burial Ground. Steps lead up the hillside to the burial ground which contains a number of old burial enclosures including Alexander Innes who rebuilt Coxton Tower. Unusually, the war memorial can be found half way up the steps. The memorial is in the form of a Gothic arch with a central panel on which the names of the fallen in the First World War were cut. It was unveiled on Sunday, 12 December 1920 by Colonel Charles James Johnston of Lesmurdie (1845–1940). There was no speech. Colonel Johnston felt too overcome by emotion and instead simply withdrew the Union Jack to unveil the memorial.

Garmouth road bears left uphill and the affluent character of the village continues along the main road to Fochabers. Cherry Cottage at the junction, the retirement home of John Cran (1820–93), banker and grain merchant, and his wife Isabella Milne McWilliam (1847–1913), and Templand Farm steading, the low building fourth from the camera, are both shown on the first edition of the 25 inch to the mile Ordnance Survey map [Elginshire sheet XIII.2] which was surveyed in 1871. The other houses date from Edwardian times and many of the first owners had small businesses such as William Taylor (1849–1921), druggist and famous for the fossil collection that he kept in his house (The Cypress), and William Mercer (1872–1954) ironmonger in Johannesburg and Elgin (Troyville), while John Cleland (1861–1932, Woodview) was a retired farmer.

Walker's Crescent, Lhanbryde

There are twelve cottages in Walker's Terrace which is a narrow lane off the Garmouth road where all the properties have long front gardens. The cottages were built when the village was formed in the 1850s and the lane is named after Robert Walker (1792–1881) of Leuchars House, the estate factor who played an important role in the re-development of Lhanbryde, the results of which were widely admired. As early as 1856, it was said that there was not a prettier village between Aberdeen and John O' Groats. This certainly contrasts with the huge local authority estates that were planned in the 1960s when Lhanbryde was chosen as the location for new high density housing. Fifty years later, a verdict on these planning decisions was given by Walker and Woodworth in their architectural guide *Aberdeenshire: North and Moray*: 'Once quite picturesque, [Lhanbryde is] now engulfed by bad modern housing to the N and E'.

In the nineteenth century Blackhills House was a shooting lodge on the extensive Fife estates and enjoyed views over the coastal plain to the Moray Firth and Sutherland Hills. The house which dates from 1837–38 had attractive gardens and in 1913 it was purchased along with the Blackhills estate from the trustees of the Duke of Fife by Thomas North Christie (1852–1939) who had retired from Ceylon (Sri Lanka) where he was involved in the tea and rubber trade. He lived at Blackhills with his sister and spent much of his free time in developing the rhododendron gardens. His nephew, Sylvester Falconer Christie (1914–83), inherited the estate in 1952 and reclaimed more land. The gardens were open in conjunction with the Scotland's Gardens Scheme and in 1993 visitors could enjoy the sight of a rare violet rhododendron in flower. The house was badly damaged in a fire in November 2015 and its present owners hope to have it rebuilt by 2020.

Coxton House and Tower is located only a short distance south of the A96 and the railway line between Aberdeen and Inverness. The fortified tower house is an A-listed building and an armorial tablet above the entrance gives the completion date as 1644. It replaced an earlier tower house that was destroyed by fire during a family dispute in the late sixteenth century. Not surprisingly perhaps, the laird Alexander Innes used as much stone in the rebuilding as possible. The massive walls are four and a half feet thick and J. and W. Watson in *Moray Described* noted that '… excepting its two external doors, which were backed by massive gates of cross-barred iron, no wood whatever was used in the whole building. It was last inhabited towards the end of the nineteenth century.' The building on the left is the Forrester's Lodge, designed by the Elgin-based architects Alexander and William Reid in 1867.

LHANBRYDE

The Innes Estate was another former Fife property. The purchaser, in 1899, was Thomas Mackenzie (1848–1915) of Dailuaine House, Carron. Mackenzie's father had founded Dailuaine Distillery in 1851 and he expanded the business by acquiring other distilleries including Talisker on Skye, Bon Accord at Aberdeen and Imperial on Speyside. One of his interests was fishing and Loch na Bo with its house close by may well have attracted him. Although he made many improvements to the estate he did not stay long and in 1912 there was another owner, Francis John Tennant (1861–1942) of Hyndford House, North Berwick, who was the brother-in-law of Prime Minister Herbert Asquith. Like many of the new owners of northern estates, Tennant was an industrialist, in his case connected with soap manufacturing. He spent part of each year at Innes and latterly lived at Loch na Bo House, where he is said to have enjoyed walking through his lands and meeting the tenants.

LHANBRYDE

Urquhart consists of a single street at the eastern end of which is the Free Church. The village was planned in 1783 by the Earl of Fife with long narrow fields (lotted lands) on either side of the main street at a time of food shortage in the North East. It became a community of tradesmen and farm workers who lived in single-storey cottages that originally had thatched roofs. The population was never large and peaked in 1871 before falling away due to the depressed conditions in agriculture that led to emigration and migration to larger towns in the south. The children on the left are standing at the entrance to the school. This closed in December 1966 and the pupils transferred to the new school at Lhanbryde. Around this time Urquhart was also handicapped by its stock of old housing and a lack of investment in services. As a consequence the village continued to stagnate and the 1971 census recorded a population of only 149.

URQUHART

Village of Urquhart

I. D. Yeadon, Elgin.

Only one house in Urquhart was re-built in the classic architectural style of the mid or late Victorian period which combined shop premises with living accommodation on the first floor. When this photograph was taken just before the First World War the merchant's business was run by John Morrison Sime (1870–1961), a postman who had married Jessie (1867–1961) the daughter of the previous owner William Munro (1836–91). Making a living in such a small community was challenging and Munro's predecessor James Coull was sequestrated in 1889 and left the district. In contrast John and Jessie Sime together with their daughters were a highly successful team who continued in business until 1967, meriting the attention of the *Northern Scot* when Urquhart was featured on 23 November 1960. The shop, which was the last one in the village, closed in 1983.

URQUHART

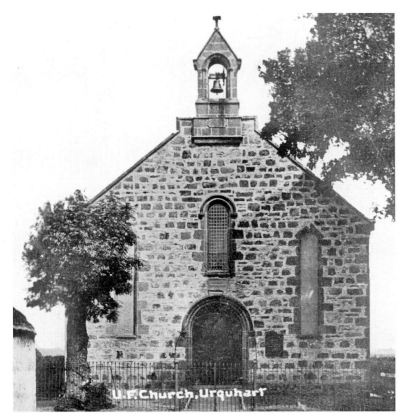

U.F.Church,Urquhart

Following the Disruption in 1843, the Established Church built a new parish church north of the village. However, the Free Church congregation was prevented from occupying the old parish church by an interdict of the Court of Session raised by the Duke of Richmond and Gordon. As a consequence a new Free Church was completed in 1844 after the purchase of stone and other materials from the old parish church. Re-unification with the Church of Scotland in 1929 resulted in the union of the two congregations in November 1937. Between 1844 and 1937 there were only two ministers, the charismatic Rev. James Morrison (1816–99), a major force in the Free Presbytery of Elgin who served the community until 1893, and his successor the Rev. Alexander Chalmers Smith (1865–1940). The church was sold in 1951 and is now a house.

The Free Church manse is set back on the north side of Main Street and reached by a driveway flanked by extensive gardens. It was built in 1846 and in 1894 it was decided that renovation and repairs were needed. The following year a bazaar was held in the Public School which was decorated for the occasion. There were stalls selling fancy goods, pictures and clothing and a provision and flower stall. A shooting gallery was set up in the playground and the competition for the prize of a pig was said to have been exciting. Two concerts in the evening rounded off the day's proceedings and visitors from town were able to catch the express train due in Elgin at 9.38 p.m. which stopped specially for them! The manse was occupied by the minister until the former Free Church and the Parish Church became a united charge in 1937 and six years later it was sold.

The Manse, Urquhart.   Published by J.M.Sime.

The coast line of the Great North of Scotland Railway from Elgin to Buckie and Portsoy opened to goods traffic on 5 April 1886 and a few weeks later to passenger trains. The *Moray and Nairn Express* on 8 May described how 'All along the coast of the Firth … the day was celebrated as the most important one in the history of the district'. People living in villages like Urquhart, Garmouth and Spey Bay thought that the completion of the 25 miles of mainly single track railway would reduce isolation, increase trade and bring prosperity to their communities. The wooden station building was typical of smaller stations on the line with the adjacent goods yard containing three sidings. Like most rail services in the North East it was a victim of the 'Beeching report' and closed on Saturday, 6 May 1968. Today there is no trace of the former station site which is now occupied by two houses one of which is called Rail-End House.

There are panoramic views from the high ground of the Browlands towards the Spey and lower Garmouth. Buildings in this photograph beginning on the left are Duncan's foundry where iron and brass were forged for ship's fittings. Next are the Free Church School (1849), converted to a hall in 1884, and the Red Lion Hotel, the principal inn in the mid-nineteenth century when it was in the hands of veteran local landlady, Margaret Syers (c. 1776–1852). Later in the century, trade suffered with the closure of most of the maritime industries and the demise of the inn was complete when its owner was declared bankrupt in 1916 and it became a private house. The large building known as the Corff House was originally used for curing salmon and storing fishing gear and served as a Territorial Army Drill Hall between 1906 and 1963 when it became the village hall for Garmouth and Kingston.

GARMOUTH

Garmouth School and River Spey.

Garmouth School is situated on high ground and a new road connected it to the village. It was officially opened on 15 May 1876 by Alexander Hay of Trochelhill, chairman of the Speymouth School Board when a procession of 200 children headed by the local volunteer band marched from Kingston to the school and the day was observed as a holiday in Garmouth. The *Elgin Courant* described the building by Reid and Melvin, architects of Elgin and Inverness, as '… handsome, substantial, and complete, built of concrete … rendered specially expedient in a place like Garmouth, which is so far from building material'. The school served the community for more than 90 years before closing on 29 March 1968. After the Easter holidays the pupils moved to the new Mosstodloch Primary School about two and a half miles away. In the early 1970s the school buildings were converted into a house and are still there today.

Bridge over the Spey, Spey Bay.

The crossing of the Spey was achieved by the Great North of Scotland Railway's longest bridge with a main span of 347 feet and three 100 feet sections on either side. The absence of rock foundations here required massive pillars to be sunk to support the bridge and because the Spey when full ran in three channels much excavation of the river bed was required upstream to ensure that the main channel passed under the central span. The viaduct cost £40,000 to construct, almost one-seventh of the Banffshire Coast line's total capital costs. When opened the railway did much to connect communities on both banks of the Spey and among other improvements it meant that post now arrived at Garmouth railway station. Although the railway closed in 1968, the bridge remains open to walkers and cyclists using the Speyside Way.

This attractive view was taken from the eighteenth century Garmouth Hotel looking towards The Cross. There have been several changes here: the cottage on the left has been cleared to make way for a car park and the boot and shoe shop has also been demolished. Both can be seen on an estate plan of 1809 and the shop was described in the Inland Revenue survey of 1913 as a very old property. This shop, together with the adjacent two-storey house, St Crispin, of which only the garden and one chimney stack are visible, was owned by William Findlater (1873–1928), shoemaker, who sadly fell to his death when carrying out repairs to his property. After this, the shop was rented to the last shoemaker in Garmouth, Charles Sievewright, who died in 1959.

CHURCH STREET, GARMOUTH

Garmouth is only three miles from the main Aberdeen to Inverness road but in the era before mass car ownership there would have been few vehicles to disturb the quiet here. In fact the only vehicles in the photographs of Garmouth are to be found outside the post office in Church Street. After the Second World War, Owen John Lewis Nash (1905–63), a new postmaster who had served in the Merchant Navy, bought the shop, former bakery and adjacent cottage (out of view) following the death of Alexander Young Smith whose family had been the village bakers since the late nineteenth century. When the popular Nash died, James Marnoch (1927–77), a local man, became postmaster until the business was sold in January 1977, eight months before his death.

Thomas Edwin and Evelyn Rose Radley from Elgin purchased the post Office and the adjacent Post Office Cottage in February 1977 and this photograph was taken eight months later. Radley was a former chief petty officer in the Royal Navy. Their tenure lasted until January 1985 when they moved to Colchester. Three more postmasters came and went before the shop was acquired by Ian Farquhar Taylor in July 1992; he advertised that his Spar shop could bring 'city shopping right to their doorsteps'. The post office was voted the best shop in Grampian in a competition jointly organized by Calor Gas and Woman and Home magazine and in 1997 the premises were refurbished and now traded as a Mace store open ninety hours per week. By then it was also the last shop in the village. In 2000 Taylor took up a role with Aberness Foods, a food wholesaler and distributor, and the Garmouth shop was operated as a franchise. In more recent times both post office and store have closed and in November 2014 the shop re-opened as Etticut Hairdressing.

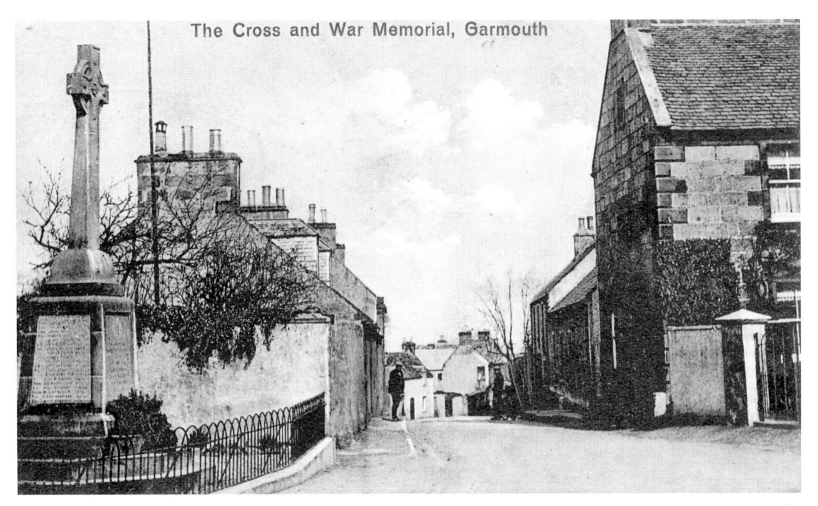

The Cross and War Memorial, Garmouth

The war memorial is situated at The Cross where three streets meet. A Celtic cross made using stone from the Newton quarries near Elgin, it was unveiled on 5 June 1921 by the Duke of Richmond and Gordon. Large numbers of local people were present on a fine Sunday afternoon when about 40 ex-servicemen lined up in front of the memorial. After the Duke had spoken of the courage of those who fought in the war and of his hopes for the younger generation he unveiled the memorial by drawing aside the Union Jack. As was customary on these occasions 'The Flowers of the Forest' was played and after the 'Last Post' was sounded John Smith, chairman of the War Memorial Committee, laid a wreath. After this the assembled servicemen filed past, each saluting and dropping a laurel leaf beside the wreath.

THE CROSS, GARMOUTH

D 2396

This Valentine postcard looks towards the High Street with the property owned by members of the Hitchcock family (page 46) visible behind the war memorial. When the photograph was taken, the merchant's shop was owned by Margaret Isabella Wright of Garmouth and Ruby Lena Gale of Kingston who ran this business between 1955 and 1964. To the right is Poplar Cottage where Donald Scott (1867–1929), tailor and clothier was the tenant. The sign on the gable end reads Scott Brothers and for a time it was known as Scott Cottage. Family members continued to live there until the death of his daughters Eva and Flora in the early 1970s. The adjacent property, partly hidden by the tree, is The Moorings, named by Captain John Geddie Spence (1873–1953), son of James Spence (1829–1902) who was an earlier owner of the merchant's shop at The Cross.

In the foreground of this photograph of High Street is the shop and former post office owned by James Hitchcock (*c.* 1833–1904). He began his working life in the timber trade, managing the sawmill owned by Colin Mackenzie & Company which cut the wood floated down the River Spey from the Glenmore Forest. When that trade went into recession he started a merchant's business and became postmaster in the mid-1870s. He was succeeded by his son John (1859–1939) but after he retired in 1930 the shop was rented by various businesses including James Davidson, draper from Portsoy, and Lewis Fraser (1895–1955), butcher, whose death and that of John Hitchcock's widow, Mary Macpherson, led to the property being sold in 1955 to George Halliday Henderson (1910–74), a butcher in Rothes.

GARMOUTH

While previous photographs have captured Garmouth's unique atmosphere of narrow streets, this view taken from a footpath off Spey Street highlights the random layout of housing in the old town. On the horizon are the Free Church (1845), boasting fine Gothic features, and the manse which was completed some five years afterwards. The church was renovated in 1893, became the parish church at re-unification in 1929, and in the early 1990s was converted into a house. The Garmouth Hotel, formerly the Star Inn and the last surviving inn from the town's seafaring days, can be found nearby at the junction of Church Street and Station Road.

Garmouth Station on the Coast line was built with two platforms, signal boxes at each end and a passenger overbridge. There was also a small goods yard. The cottage in the distance is the stationmaster's house. These features can be seen on the 25 inch to the mile Ordnance Survey map [Elginshire sheet 009.09] which was revised in 1903. The decommissioning of the signal box and second platform had occurred before the second photograph was taken in 1960. In another eight years the railway closed and the track was lifted. The station building was used for a time by a youth club while the surrounding area remained in a derelict state. After purchase by Moray District Council in 1983 the station site was landscaped with some land being developed for sheltered housing which became known as The Sidings.

Kingston and Garmouth were important maritime communities throughout the nineteenth century when timber from the forests of Speyside was used to build ships. The banks of the Spey were lined with shipbuilding yards and sawmills. From right to left can be seen the eastern part of Beach Road (page 50), the ship building yard of the Glenmore Company (which was later owned by the Duncan family as was the Red Corff House, also known as Dunfermline House) and a former steam-powered sawmill. Towards the left is Millbank House which was owned by James Geddie (1809–82), whose family were ship owners as well as being involved in the timber trade and shipbuilding.

Kingston consists of four rows of houses running on an east-west axis roughly parallel with the shore. The corner shop on Beach Road was owned by William Geddie (1835–1907) whose father James Geddie was a well-known shipbuilder. Geddie traded for nearly forty years as a general merchant and ship's chandler. The adjacent corrugated iron storage shed, just visible, is on the Marine Hotel plot. Owned by Charles Shand (1839–97), painter, the hotel opened in 1885 when the first tenant was Patrick Weir (1818–1909), a former wine merchant. Unfortunately, the hotel was destroyed by fire on a windy night in November 1889 after another tenant overturned a paraffin lamp in the bar. The villagers prevented the blaze from spreading to William Geddie's house and shop.

The southern flank of Kingston was known as Front Row (later Lein Road) and has a south-facing aspect overlooking open countryside. There are several stone-built houses with large gardens where wealthier families lived. The first house on the left, Lynnside, had been owned by William Hustwick (1778–1868), shipbuilder and ship owner, and was purchased by John Bale (1828–1910), a retired supervisor in the Inland Revenue. In 1910 the next four houses belonged to: Alexandra Spence (1867–1936), daughter of Alexander Anderson, master mariner (Plum Villa); Ann Geddie (1821–1910) widow of John Duncan, ship owner (The Yews); William Kinloch (1836–1911), shipbuilder (Sunnybank); and Ann Ironside Runcie (1836–1914), widow of William Marr, master mariner (Seaview). The house on Middle Row facing the camera is the rebuilt Marine Hotel (page 50). This was run by Charles Shand's wife, Janet Henderson Marshall (1840–1923), until 1914.

This view from close to the western extremity of Front Row highlights the pebble and gorse strewn terrain and the homes of those employed in the shipbuilding trades. The two-storey property known as The Villas was built for Alexander Ritchie (1851–1922), son of local dairymaid Isabella Smith, who worked as a ship's carpenter in Kingston before qualifying for his master's certificate. He lived in Mauritius in the early 1890s where he married Marjory Smith from Buckie and two children were born. After returning to Aberdeen, he had The Villas built on old house plots in 1901 and the first occupants were his mother and half-sister Jane Simpson. The property was lived in for a time by Alexina Mary Smith (1869–1965), who taught at Garmouth School, and after Ritchie's death ownership passed to his daughter, Mary Easton Ritchie (1894–1969).

This photograph looks east over much of the village. On the extreme right can be seen the houses along Front Row with Dunfermline House (page 49) slightly to the left in the distance. Among the cottages thatched roofs are beginning to give way to slate and iron. The gardens contain various wooden huts and although there are a few stone walls made from boulders brought down by the Spey, many of the gardens were enclosed with wooden fences. These would probably have been made using offcuts from the local sawmills. The soil to make the gardens was carted from the nearby saltings while some was brought into the port as ballast.

　　KINGSTON

Spey Bay Post Office.

In February 1911 postal workers Mary (1874–1947) and Jeannie (1879–1931) Watson bought land at the junction of the Fochabers–Spey Bay and Nether Dallachy roads and built a new house and post office known as Castleview. The location was convenient for the railway station (visible in the distance) and the emerging golfing resort of Spey Bay. The Watson family had long connections with postal services: William Watson (1834–1908) was postmaster, merchant and horse hirer when the office was in Nether Dallachy half a mile away, while Jeannie was a sorting clerk and telegraphist for a time at Buckie. After Jeannie's marriage and emigration to Canada in 1912, Mary and her brother William (1872–1950) worked at the post office until the mid-1940s and following several changes of ownership the shop was rented by Ian Taylor who also ran post offices at Garmouth (page 43) and Urquhart. The post office closed twenty years ago and the shop windows and entrance on the gable end of the building have been filled in.

SPEY BAY

When the Coast line opened in 1886 the station here was called Fochabers-on-Spey, reflecting the nearest important village. At that time the coast at this point was largely unpopulated, with the road north leading only to the salmon fishing station at Tugnet close to the mouth of the River Spey. After further name changes in 1893 (Fochabers) and 1916 (Fochabers and Spey Bay), the station became known as Spey Bay on 1 January 1918. During this time, a hotel, golf course and a number of houses overlooking the Moray Firth were built and Spey Bay became a fashionable small-scale holiday resort. Like Urquhart Station (page 37), there was a goods yard behind the station building which closed in April 1964. The passing loop and signal box were removed in 1966 and the last passenger services were on 6 May 1968 when the Coast line closed. The building and platform have survived and are a feature of the much extended gardens of the station cottage.

SPEY BAY

178   RICHMOND GORDON HOTEL, SPEY BAY

The Spey Bay Hotel was designed by Cameron and Watt, architects of Aberdeen, for Mary Bruce Hutchison (1865–1937) who owned the Richmond Café in the city. The hotel opened in 1907, the same year as the golf course. It was so successful in its first season that during the winter of 1908–09 further building work was completed which doubled the size of the hotel. Initially, the hotel was lit by petrol gas lamps and it converted to electricity in 1919. In 1928 it was sold to Harry H. Ward (1872–1949), owner of the Queensgate Hotel in Inverness and a keen golfer. The hotel, which became well-known throughout Scotland as a golfing and fishing centre, was closed for the winter when it was destroyed by fire in January 1965. The building on the left of the picture is the clubhouse of Spey Bay Golf Club which opened in 1913.

THE SHORE ROAD, SPEY BAY.

A.2579.

The 25 inch to the mile Ordnance Survey map [Elginshire sheet 009.05] which was surveyed in 1903 shows only four houses on the Shore Road east of Tugnet. In this 1935 view housing now extends all the way to the hotel in the distance. The new golf course had an immediate impact: in 1906 plots for two villas were sold by the Richmond and Gordon Estates and applications for a further two sites were received. Just beyond the motor car is a semi-detached property built in 1910; nearest the camera is The Rest, originally owned by James Hay Marshall (1870–1935), architect for the Richmond and Gordon Estates, and next door is The Mouries which first belonged to Charles Gray (1849–1927), bank agent in Fochabers. The houses on this road attracted retired people or were purchased as holiday homes.